To: _____

From: _____

I Had a Great Teacher

A CELEBRATION OF THOSE WHO EDUCATE AND INSPIRE

by Kathy Wagoner

GRAMERCY BOOKS
New York

This 2003 edition is published by Gramercy Books, an imprint of
Random House Value Publishing, a division of Random House, Inc., New York
by arrangement with Sourcebooks, Inc.

Gramercy Books is a registered trademark and
the colophon is a trademark of Random House, Inc.

Interior Design: Karen Ocker Design, New York

Previously published under the title *365 Appleseeds: A Grateful Gift for Teachers.*

Random House
New York • Toronto • London • Sydney • Auckland
www.randomhouse.com/

Library of Congress Cataloging-in-Publication Data

365 appleseeds
    I had a great teacher : a celebration of those who educate and inspire /
[compiled] by Kathy Wagoner.
        p. cm.
    Originally published: 365 appleseeds. Naperville, Ill. : Sourcebooks, 2001.
    ISBN 0-517-22184-5
        1. Education—Quotations, maxims, etc. I. Wagoner, Kathy. II. Title.

PN6084.E38 A17 2003
370—dc21

                                                                2002029416

9 8 7 6 5 4 3 2 1

Introduction

In one way or another, each of us is a
teacher. A few people, however, devote
their lives to this noble profession. They
share of themselves so that others may
grow and learn. This book provides
thanks and encouragement
to those teachers
in our lives.

A teacher affects eternity;
no one can tell where
his influence stops.

Henry Adams

The potential of a child is the most intriguing
and stimulating thing in all creation.

Ray L. Wilbur

The long journey toward the end of the chapter
begins with a short step into that first paragraph.

It is in identifying yourself with the hopes,
dreams, fears and longings of others that you
may understand them and help them.

Wilferd A. Peterson

What we hope ever to do with ease,
we must learn first to do with diligence.

Samuel Johnson

Recognize achievement every day.
Reward responsibility every hour.

Education has for its object the formation of character.

Herbert Spencer

Experience is the name that everyone gives to his mistakes.

Oscar Wilde

Every person is gifted in some area.
We just have to find out what.

Evelyn Blose Holman

Listening is the shortest distance between two people.

The man who does not read good books has no
advantage over the man who cannot read them.

Mark Twain

If you always do what you always did,
you'll always get what you always got.

Verne Hill

I touch the future. I teach.

Christa McAuliffe

He who praises everybody praises nobody.

Samuel Johnson

Lucky is the teacher whose students
want to know how things work.

Reading maketh a full man, conference a ready
man, and writing an exact man.

Francis Bacon

Nothing is so strong as gentleness;
nothing so gentle as real strength.

St. Francis de Sales

Training means learning the rules.
Experience means learning the exceptions.

Maturing is the process by which the individual
becomes conscious of the equal importance
of each of his fellow men.

Alvin Goeser

That I may care enough to love enough to share enough to
let others become what they can be.

John O'Brien

What sculpture is to a block of marble,
education is to a human soul.

Joseph Addison

The cost of educating a child today is immense.
But the cost of not educating a child is incalculable.

The mind is master of the man, and so
"they can who think they can."

Nixon Waterman

A book should teach us to enjoy life, or to endure it.

Samuel Johnson

The scholar who cherishes the love of comfort
is not fit to be deemed a scholar.

Confucius

Just think of the tragedy of teaching
children not to doubt.

Clarence Darrow

The mind can absorb only what the seat can endure.

Children are our most valuable natural resource.

Herbert Hoover

Every great man is always being helped by everybody;
for his gift is to get good out of all things and all persons.

John Ruskin

If we were supposed to talk more than we listen,
we would have two mouths and one ear.

Mark Twain

I am not a teacher—only a fellow traveler of whom you
asked the way. I pointed ahead—ahead of myself
as well as of you.

George Bernard Shaw

If at first you don't succeed, don't worry because
neither did the teacher in the next classroom.

You must never tell a thing. You must illustrate it.
We learn through the eye and not the noggin.

Will Rogers

The right angle to solve a difficult problem is the "try-angle."

Ellis I. Levitt

One of a student's biggest fears is not being listened to.

A master can tell you what he expects of you.
A teacher, though, awakens your own expectations.

Patricia Neal

The one exclusive sign of thorough
knowledge is the power of teaching.

Aristotle

*C*hild, give me your hand
that I may walk in the light
of your faith in me.

Hannah Kahn

If you make two people in your classroom
happy today, be sure one of them is you.

The art of teaching is
the art of assisting discovery.

Mark Van Doren

A student who tries something and fails is better
than a student who does nothing and succeeds.

An error of opinion may be tolerated where
reason is left free to combat it.

Thomas Jefferson

Misinformation is one of the greatest
dangers of modern education.

Charles F. Kettering

Lucky is the teacher who can look across
the room and not see one bored face.

The object of teaching a child is to enable him
to get along without his teacher.

Elbert Hubbard

Our greatest glory consists not in never falling,
but in rising every time we fall.

Oliver Goldsmith

Knowledge is the eye of desire and
can become the pilot of the soul.

Will Durant

Men, in teaching others, learn themselves.

Seneca

Be patient with your students.
The rate may be slow, but the growth is immense!

They are ill discoverers that think there is no land,
when they can see nothing but sea.

Francis Bacon

Answer me in one word.

William Shakespeare

Education is helping the child realize his potentialities.

Erich Fromm

What the teacher is, is more important
than what he teaches.

Karl Menninger

The true aim of everyone who aspires to be a teacher should be, not to impart his own opinion, but to kindle minds.

A person who cannot read knows only what he is told.

Thinking is the hardest work there is.

Henry Ford

Teaching for tests creates learnoids.

Alan Scott Winston

The object of education is to prepare the young to educate themselves throughout their lives.

Robert Maynard Hutchins

A chain is only as strong as its weakest link, and to limit teaching to the lowest level of understanding does not make the chain any stronger.

Teaching is fun.

Jaime Escalante

Music training is a more potent instrument than
any other, because rhythm and harmony find
their way into the inward places of the soul.

Plato

In teaching, it is the method and not
the content that is the message…the
drawing out, not the pumping in.

Ashley Montagu

Your student's successes are ultimately your own.

A wise man's heart guides his mouth,
and his lips promote instruction.

Proverbs 16:23 (NIV)

Everyone is ignorant, only
on different subjects.

Will Rogers

Anytime you see a turtle up on top
of a fence post, you know he had some help.

Alex Haley

Expect your students to be winners.
Expect your students to be the best.

He that revels in a well-chosen library has
innumerable dishes and all of admirable flavor.

William Godwin

We know what we are, but not what we may be.

William Shakespeare

Experience is the child of thought
and thought is the child of action.

Benjamin Disraeli

When you help someone up a hill, you're that
much nearer the top yourself.

Train a child in a way he should go; and
when he is old, he will not turn from it.

Proverbs 22:6 (NIV)

Don't let failure go to your head.

Haim Ginott

The teacher is like a candle that lights others
at the risk of consuming itself.

How the children turn out will depend
on what we put into the effort.

Lottie Taylor

Blessed is the influence of one true,
loving human soul on another.

George Eliot

There is one thing stronger than all the armies in the
world, and that is an idea whose time has come.

Victor Hugo

Come what come may, Time and the
hour runs through the roughest day.

Teachers make hope happen.

No student knows his subject. The most he knows is
where and how to find out the things he does not know.

Woodrow Wilson

Intelligence defies fate.
So long as a man can think, he is free.

Ralph Waldo Emerson

If a man empties his purse into his head, no man
can take it from him. An investment in knowledge
always pays the best interest.

Benjamin Franklin

Knowledge comes, but wisdom lingers.

Alfred, Lord Tennyson

A man should learn to sail in all winds.

Italian proverb

A teacher is one who, in his youth, admired teachers.

H. L. Mencken

Patience is the ability to idle your motor
when you feel like stripping your gears.

The teacher is one who makes two ideas
grow where only one grew before.

Elbert Hubbard

We need to make education a community obsession.

Joan Kowal

Knowledge exists to be imparted.

Ralph Waldo Emerson

Science is simply common sense at its best.

T. H. Huxley

Education is what survives when what has
been learned has been forgotten.

B. F. Skinner

The most complicated concept can be mastered
by breaking it down into small parts.

You have to be either critically loving or a loving critic,
but you should never be indifferent.

John Gardner

Example is always more efficacious than precept.

Samuel Johnson

I have the basic belief that all children can learn.
Our expectation is that they will.

Carol Purvis

Better three hours too soon than a minute too late.

William Shakespeare

He who wrestles with us strengthens our
nerves and sharpens our skills.

Edward Burke

Better to do a little well than a great deal poorly.
Life's greatest adventure is in doing one's level best.

Arthur Morgan

Education is the ticket to success.

Jaime Escalante

To have inspired a student to become the person he
wants to be is a teacher's greatest achievement.

We speak of educating our children.
Do we know that our children educate us?

Lydia Sigourney

Chaos often breeds life,
where order breeds but habit.

Henry Adams

A good education teaches a student what to remember
from the past, what to enjoy in the present, and
what to plan for in the future.

Recognize differences. Don't alter your
expectations, but alter your approach.

Annie Benford Duvall

I teach with my heart and my soul and not with my mouth alone.

Jaime Escalante

Wouldn't it be wonderful if people valued
education as much as they value schooling?

The mediocre teacher tells.
The good teacher explains. The
superior teacher demonstrates.
The great teacher inspires.

William Arthur Ward

For he that was only taught by himself
had a fool for a master.

Ben Jonson

Education is growth.

John Dewey

An error is not a terror.

Haim Ginott

We're here to help children succeed.
It's that simple.

Elaine Collins

The secret of education lies in respecting the pupil.

Ralph Waldo Emerson

In the garden of learning, the seeds that
are planted today will produce tomorrow's harvest.

This will never be a civilized country until we spend
more money for books than we do for chewing gum.

Elbert Hubbard

Great works are preformed not
by strength but by perseverance.

Samuel Johnson

Be strong enough so that nothing can disturb your peace
of mind…not even a paper airplane that sails across the
back of the room while you are speaking.

Children have more need of models than of critics.

Joseph Joubert

Difficult: that which can be done immediately.
Impossible: that which takes a little longer.

George Santayana

It is easier to move a cemetery than to effect a
change in curriculum.

Woodrow Wilson

A child miseducated is a child lost.

John F. Kennedy

I beg of you to stop apologizing for being a member
of the most important profession in the world.

William G. Carr

The president of the United States fifty years from now is
sitting in a classroom, being taught, being inspired;
and she is having a good day.

To accomplish great things, we must not only act but also
dream, not only plan but also believe.

Anatole France

Difficulties strengthen the mind, as labor does the body.

Seneca

A classroom full of students is like a team.
Everyone needs to work together to win the game.

Learning is like rowing upstream—not
to advance is to drop back.

Chinese proverb

The man who can make hard things easy is the educator.

Ralph Waldo Emerson

Treat people as if they were what they ought to be, and you help them to become what they are capable of being.

Johann Von Goethe

There is a destiny that makes us brothers; none goes his way alone: All that we send into the lives of others comes back into our own.

Edwin Markham

I find that a great part of the information I have was acquired by looking up something else on the way.

Franklin P. Adams

Even the gifted and talented student needs help, support, and encouragement to succeed.

Consider the postage stamp. Its usefulness consists in
the ability to stick to one thing until it gets there.

Josh Billings

Few things help an individual more than to place responsibility upon him, and to let him know that you trust him.

Booker T. Washington

He that has patience may compass anything.

Francois Rabelais

Natural abilities are like natural plants;
they need pruning by study.

Francis Bacon

I am always ready to learn, but I
do not always like being taught.

Winston Churchill

Failing to prepare is preparing to fail.

Anonymous

More matter, with less art.

William Shakespeare

Vast numbers of Americans rely as much on astrology as
on astronomy. We have a way to go in education.

Stephanie Pace Marshall

People who aren't in education just don't know what
they're missing.

Keith Blue

A minute's success pays for the years of failure.

Robert Browning

New knowledge grows from the seeds
of what is already known.

Those who educate children well are more to be honored
than even their parents, for these only give them life;
those the art of living well.

Aristotle

After the verb "to love," "to help"
is the most beautiful verb in the world.

Bertha von Suttner

The hardest part about being a good
teacher is that you have to do it every day.

The foundation of every state
is the education of its youth.

Diogenes

The system of classifying students as "special needs," "at risk," or "talented and gifted" fails to recognize that all students are unique.

By learning you will teach, by teaching you will learn.

Latin proverb

It is greater work to educate a child, in the true and larger sense of the word, than to rule a state.

William Ellery Channing

Our progress as a nation can be no swifter than our progress in education.

John F. Kennedy

When a teacher really gets to know a student, a partnership is created that allows learning to be accomplished.

That's what learning is.
You suddenly understand
something you've understood
all your life, but in a new way.

Doris Lessing

We teachers can only help the work going on,
as servants wait upon a master.

Maria Montessori

'Tis education forms the common mind,
just as the twig is bent, the tree's inclined.

Alexander Pope

To teach is to learn twice.

Joseph Joubert

Education is a better safeguard of liberty
than a standing army.

Edward Everett

Children have to be educated, but they
have also to be left to educate themselves.

Abbé Dimnet

Happy is he who has been able
to learn the causes of things.

Virgil

Knowledge is the true organ of sight, not the eyes.

Panchatantra

Education is not the filling of a pail,
but the lighting of a fire.

William Butler Yeats

Teachers give all that they are able
to persuade their students to take.

One looks back with appreciation to the brilliant teachers,
but with gratitude to those who touched our human feelings.

Carl Jung

Education is a wonderful thing. If you couldn't
sign your name, you'd have to pay cash.

Rita Mae Brown

Education is the best provision for old age.

Aristotle

The end and aim of all education
is the development of character.

Francis W. Parker

It was my teacher's genius, her quick sympathy, her loving
tact which made the first years of my education so beautiful.

Helen Keller

Good teaching is one-fourth
preparation and three-fourths theater.

Gail Godwin

Education makes people easy to lead, but difficult to
drive; easy to govern, but impossible to enslave.

Henry Peter Brougham

If you are a teacher you can change the world because it's your
world. You can have an influence on your sphere, your domain.

Senator Barbara Mikulski

Surely, therefore, the very nature and needs of the contemporary
world make the teacher an indispensable member of society.

Calvin O. Davis

If we would have new knowledge,
we must get a world of new questions.

Susan Langer

You don't understand anything until
you learn it more than one way.

Marvin Minsky

Education is the taming of domestication of the soul's
raw passions—not suppressing them or excising them,
which would deprive the soul of its energy—but forming
and informing them as art.

Allan Bloom

Education is freedom.

André Gide

Seeing a child's successful progress during the school
year confirms a teacher's calling to the profession.

Education must have an end in view,
for it is not an end in itself.

Sybil Marshall

It made me gladsome to be getting some education,
it being like a big window opening.

Mary Webb

Memorizing facts does little to teach how
to achieve desired results.

But need alone is not enough to set
power free: there must be knowledge.

Ursula K. Le Guin

We have a hunger of the mind which asks for knowledge
of all around us, and the more we gain, the more is our
desire; the more we see, the more are we capable of seeing.

Maria Mitchell

It is not only by the questions we have answered that progress may be measured, but also by those we are still asking. The passionate controversies of one era are viewed as sterile preoccupations by another, for knowledge alters what we seek as well as what we find.

Freda Adler

Worlds can be found by a child and an adult bending down and looking together under the grass stems or at the skittering crabs in a tidal pool.

Mary Catherine Bateson

Everything is data. But data isn't everything.

Pauline Bart

One can learn, at least. One can go on learning until the day one is cut off.

Fay Weldon

The joy of learning is as indispensable
in study as breathing is in running.

Simone Weil

The world of learning is so broad, and the human soul is so
limited in power! We reach forth and strain every nerve, but we
seize only a bit of the curtain that hides the infinite from us.

Maria Mitchell

The excitement of learning separates youth from old age.
As long as you're learning you're not old.

Rosalyn S. Yalow

The way to do research is to attack the facts
at the point of greatest astonishment.

Celia Green

Teaching is the royal road to learning.

Jessamyn West

If you can keep your head when all about you are losing theirs, it's just possible you haven't grasped the situation.

Jean Kerr

Using good grades as the measure of one's success in learning is meaningless if nothing is learned truly.

Knowledge advances by steps and not by leaps.

Thomas Macaulay

Education is learning what you didn't even know you didn't know.

Daniel J. Boorstin

Education is the ability to listen to almost anything without losing your temper or your self-confidence.

Robert Frost

Education should be a lifelong process, the formal
period serving as a foundation on which
life's structure may rest and rise.

Robert H. Jackson

Intelligence plus character—that
is the goal of true education.

Martin Luther King, Jr.

Until the student knows how much you care,
he won't care how much you know.

Education should consist of a series of enchantments,
each raising the individual to a higher level of awareness,
understanding, and kinship with all living things.

Anonymous

To know how to suggest is the great art of teaching.

Henri Amiel

Learn something new each day and prosper.

A teacher's major contribution may pop out anonymously
in the life of some ex-student's grandchild.

Wendell Berry

Come, give us a taste of your quality.

William Shakespeare

Teachers provide a social and intellectual
environment in which students can learn.

James MacGregor Burns

The true teacher does not teach, yet one may educate oneself
at his side; in just the same way the wise man does not
create folk culture, but it takes form naturally in his presence.

Vinoba Bhave

The teacher who walks in the shadow of the temple, among
his followers, gives not of his wisdom but rather of his faith
and his lovingness. If he is indeed wise he does not bid you
enter the house of his wisdom, but rather leads you to the
threshold of your own mind.

Kahlil Gibran

Learning is continuous, for to stop would be
like reading yesterday's newspaper forever.

It is the supreme art of the teacher to awaken
joy in creative expression and knowledge.

Albert Einstein

The greatest sign of success for a teacher…is to be able to
say, "The children are now working as if I did not exist."

Maria Montessori

When the student is ready, the teacher arrives;
when the teacher is ready, the student arrives.

Anonymous

Genius is one percent inspiration and
ninety-nine percent perspiration.

Thomas Alva Edison

Children learn to creep ere they can learn to go.

John Heywood

Teach by doing whenever you can, and only fall back
upon words when doing it is out of the question.

Rousseau

The educator is like a good gardener, whose function is to
make available healthy, fertile soil in which a young plant
can grow strong roots.

E. F. Schumacher

A teacher who can unlock a student's potential
has helped to make the world a better place.

*I*f you have knowledge, let others light their candles at it.

Margaret Fuller

Successful teachers are surpassed by their pupils.

Anonymous

Teachers open the door,
but you must enter by yourself.

Chinese proverb

A student's future occupation depends
on his or her present education.

The boughs of no two trees ever have the
same arrangement. Nature always produces
individuals; she never produces classes.

Lydia Maria Child

A student who learns from failure
will have achieved success.

One must separate from anything that forces
one to repeat "No" again and again.

Friedrich Nietzsche

The practice of "reviewing"… in general has nothing in common with the art of criticism.

Henry James

Perfection is the child of Time.

Bishop Joseph Hall

We never do anything well till we cease to think about the manner of doing it.

William Hazlitt

The force of necessity is irresistible.

Aeschylus

He who can't remember clearly his own childhood is a poor educator.

Marie von Ebner-Eschenbach

Before beginning, prepare carefully.

Cicero

You may talk too much on the best of subjects.

Benjamin Franklin

Readers are plentiful; thinkers are rare.

Harriet Martineau

My days ran away so fast. I simply ran after my days.

Leah Morton

The responsibility a dedicated teacher feels for
educating students is considerable indeed.

Those having torches will pass them on to others.

Plato

The true teacher defends his pupils
against his own personal influence.

A. B. Alcott

The rule is, jam tomorrow and jam
yesterday—but never jam today.

Lewis Carroll

I would help others, out of a fellow-feeling.

Robert Burton

Establishing lasting peace is the work of education.

Maria Montessori

History repeats itself because learning from the past
requires a longer memory than most possess.

Rome was not built in one day.

John Heywood

Woe to be him that reads but one book.

George Herbert

A great interpreter of life ought
not himself to need interpretation.

Ernst Mach

To know when one's self is interested,
is the first condition of interesting other people.

Walter Pater

The byproduct is sometimes more valuable than the product.

Havelock Ellis

There is always one moment in childhood
when the door opens and lets the future in.

Graham Greene

We shouldn't teach great books;
we should teach a love of reading.

B. F. Skinner

A teacher is one who understands that a concept can be voiced aloud, but until there is comprehension, there has been no true learning.

Mix a little foolishness with your serious plans: it's lovely to be silly at the right moment.

Horace

If a little knowledge is dangerous, where is the man who has so much as to be out of danger?

T. H. Huxley

The supreme achievement is to accomplish that which cannot be done.

You can cover a great deal of country in books.

Andrew Lang

One does not know—cannot know—the best that is in one.

Friedrich Nietzsche

There is no substitute for hard work.

Thomas Alva Edison

Tact is, after all, a kind of mind-reading.

Sarah Orne Jewett

Learn, compare, collect the facts!

Ivan Petrovich Pavlov

Only those ideas that are least truly ours
can be adequately expressed in words.

Henri Bergson

Experience, the universal Mother of Sciences.

Miguel de Cervantes

No rule is so general, which admits not some exception.

Robert Burton

Teaching someone how to think, not
what to think, is easier said than done.

Hold their noses to grindstone.

John Heywood

If you can look into the seeds of time,
And say which grain will grow and which will not,
Speak.

William Shakespeare

How shall I be able to rule over others, that
have not full power and command of myself?

François Rabelais

Since I would rather make of him (the child)
an able man than a learned man, I would also urge
that care be taken to choose a (tutor) with a
well-made rather than a well-filled head.

Michel de Montaigne

Look to the essence of a thing, whether it be a point
of doctrine, of practice, or of interpretation.

Marcus Aurelius Antoninus

A teacher wears many hats on the same day,
depending on the ever-changing needs of the students.

The chief merit of language is clearness, and we know that
nothing detracts so much from this as do unfamiliar terms.

Galen

All things are filled full of signs, and it is a wise man
who can learn about one thing from another.

Plotinus

Success and failure are intertwined. Babe Ruth led the league
in strikeouts in the same year that he hit sixty home runs.

*E*ducation is not a
preparation for life;
education is life itself.

John Dewey

No one cares to speak to an unwilling listener. An arrow never lodges in a stone: often it recoils upon the sender of it.

St. Jerome

Hear the other side.

St. Augustine

He listens well who takes notes.

Dante Alighieri

The more wise and powerful a master, the more directly is his work created, and the simpler it is.

Meister Eckhart

Reflection at the end of the day provides perspective to begin again tomorrow.

Learning without thought is labor lost; thought without learning is perilous.

Confucius

Much learning does not teach understanding.

Heraclitus

Let early education be a sort of amusement; you
will then be better able to find out the natural bent.

Plato

You cannot put the same shoe on every foot.

Publius Syrus

Nothing is so difficult but that it may be found out by seeking.

Terence (Publius Terentius Afer)

The very spring and root of honesty
and virtue lie in good education.

Plutarch

A good mind possesses a kingdom.

Seneca

The example set by others does more
to teach values than many hours of lecture.

Sometimes a person's mind is stretched by a new idea
and never does go back to its old dimensions.

Oliver Wendell Holmes

I think the necessity of being ready increases. Look to it.

Abraham Lincoln

People ask you for criticism, but they only want praise.

Somerset Maugham

The fate of the books depends on the capacity of the reader.

Terentianus Maurus

Teaching that would lay any claim at all to distinction, if
not to actual greatness, is the influence of personality upon
personality, rather than the mere imparting of a set of facts.

Frank E. Gaebelein

Education is simply the soul of a society as it
passes from one generation to another.

G. K. Chesterton

A good example can make the solution
to a complex problem clear.

Education made us what we are.

Claude-Adrian Helvetius

A child can be saved from the worst circumstances
by providing the opportunity for a good education.

I have learned since to be a better student, and to be
ready to say to my fellow students, "I do not know."

William Osler

We class schools, you see, into four grades: Leading
School, First-rate School, Good School, and School.

Evelyn Waugh

None of the great discoveries was made
by a "specialist" or a "researcher."

Martin H. Fischer

An important part of learning is to keep an open
mind—something worthwhile may drop into it.

I have never let my schooling interfere with my education.

Mark Twain

Example is the school of mankind,
and they will learn at no other.

Edmund Burke

The art of pleasing consists in being pleased.

William Hazlitt

When things are steep, remember to stay level-headed.

Horace

It is easy to be wise after the event.

Proverb

The readiness is all.

William Shakespeare

It is good to know what a man is, and also what the world
takes him for. But you do not understand him until you
have learnt how he understands himself.

F. H. Bradley

Self-reflection is the school of wisdom.

Baltasar Gracian

Have a heart that never hardens, and a temper that never
fires, and a touch that never hurts.

Charles Dickens

The person who believes he knows everything
will be passed by those who know they don't.

There are tones of voice that mean
more than words.

Robert Frost

Your own gift can present every moment with the
cumulative force of a whole life's cultivation.

Ralph Waldo Emerson

Seeing the intellectual growth of one of your students take
place before your very eyes makes some of the difficulties
associated with teaching suddenly bearable.

In case of doubt, it is better to say too little than too much.

Thomas Jefferson

I never lose an opportunity of urging a practical beginning,
however small, for it is wonderful how often in such matters
the mustard seed germinates and roots itself.

Florence Nightingale

The universe is too great a mystery for
there to be only one single approach to it.

Symmachus

What would life be without arithmetic, but a scene of horrors?

Rev. Sydney Smith

For all knowledge and wonder (which is the seed of
knowledge) is an impression of pleasure in itself.

Francis Bacon

The whole art of teaching is only the art of awakening
the natural curiosity of young minds for the
purpose of satisfying it afterwards.

Anatole France

Not only is there but one way of doing things rightly, but
there is only one way of seeing them, and that is,
seeing the whole of them.

John Ruskin

Simple as it seems, it was a great discovery that the key of
knowledge could turn both ways, that it could open, as
well as lock, the door of power to the many.

James Russell Lowell

A human being is not, in any proper sense,
a human being until he is educated.

Horace Mann

We are born for cooperation, as are the feet, the hands,
the eyelids, and the upper and lower jaws.

Marcus Aurelius Antoninus

Teachers may be underpaid and overworked, but so much
more greatly appreciated are they by those who realize
that they have learned something from them.

*H*e alone is worthy of the Appellation who either does great things, or teaches how they may be done, or describes them with a suitable majesty when they have been done.

John Milton

Nature gave men two ends—one to sit on and one to think with. Ever since then man's success or failure has been dependent on the one he used most.

George R. Kirkpatrick

Iron rusts from disuse, stagnant water loses its purity, and in cold weather becomes frozen; even so does inaction sap the vigors of the mind.

Leonardo da Vinci

Facts are stubborn things.

Alain Rene Le Sage

To teach is to guide the learner
to a place he or she has never seen.

Upon the subject of education, not presuming to dictate any plan or system respecting it, I can only say that I view it as the most important subject which we, as a people, can be engaged in.

Abraham Lincoln

Thinking leads men to knowledge. One may see and hear and read and learn as much as he pleases; he will never know any of it except that which he has thought over, that which by thinking he has made the property of his mind. Is it then saying too much if I say that man by thinking only becomes truly great?

Johann Heinrich Pestalozzi

I teach you the Superman. Man is something that is to be surpassed. What have you done to surpass him?

Friedrich Nietzsche

To understand is hard. Once one understands, action is easy.

Sun Yat-sen

Knowing the answer to a question is not as important as being able to find the answer.

Keep the golden mean between saying too much and too little.

Publius Syrus

What a teacher doesn't say is a telling part of what a student hears.

Maurice Natanson

A good teacher is one who helps you
become who you feel yourself to be.

Julius Lester

Teaching is selflessness in the service of others.

Berlie J. Fallon

To teach something you don't know is like coming
back from someplace you've never been.

Anonymous

My joy in learning is partly that it enables me to teach.

Seneca

One good teacher in a lifetime may sometimes
change a delinquent into a solid citizen.

Phillip Wylie

It is a reality that the word
"earning" is a part of "learning."

Men exist for the sake of one another.
Teach them then or bear with them.

Marcus Aurelius Antoninus

Knowledge is proud that he has learned so much;
Wisdom is humble that he knows no more.

William Cowper

Education is…hanging around until you've caught on.

Robert Frost

Often, the only praise many young children
receive is from teachers at school.

Be not afraid of growing slowly,
be afraid only of standing still.

Chinese proverb

Any subject can be taught effectively in some intellectually
honest form to any child at any stage of development.

Jerome Seymour Bruner